IMAGES
of America

AROUND
MONARCH PASS

QUICK'S HILL. Quick's Hill was located 8 miles south of Crested Butte, and like the early days on Monarch and Marshall Passes, it was used by local skiers. No lifts existed, but skiing and tobogganing began after 1915 and continued until 1940 and the beginning of the Pioneer Ski Area. Here Western State College student Fred Brand is in the air on his toboggan. (Author's collection.)

ON THE COVER: An automobile heads up the east side of Monarch Pass in 1950. Snow is piled high on both sides of the road, and the Sawatch Mountains provide a stunningly beautiful backdrop. Heavy snow, steep grades, and wind forced drivers to exercise extreme caution when traveling over Monarch Pass. (Courtesy of Western State College Collection.)

IMAGES
of America

AROUND
MONARCH PASS

Duane Vandenbusche

ARCADIA
PUBLISHING

Published by Arcadia Publishing
Charleston, South Carolina

Library of Congress Control Number: 2009943856

For all general information contact Arcadia Publishing at:
Telephone 843-853-2070
Fax 843-853-0044
E-mail sales@arcadiapublishing.com
For customer service and orders:
Toll-Free 1-888-313-2665

Visit us on the Internet at www.arcadiapublishing.com

This book is dedicated to my grandfather and grandmother, Remi and Marie Vandenbusche, who came from the Old Country—Belgium.

CONTENTS

ACKNOWLEDGMENTS

Many individuals, libraries, and museums are to be thanked for the use of photographs in this book. The Western State College, Salida, Denver Public, and Colorado State Historical Libraries were of tremendous help in tracking down and providing photographs.

Individuals who played a major role in putting together *Around Monarch Pass* include Dan Bender, Bob Nicolls, George Cowherd, and Rich Morehead of Monarch Mountain, who were very helpful with historical photographs of one of Colorado's oldest ski areas. Jack Watkins, general manager of the Monarch Mountain Ski Area for over 20 years, provided a wealth of information. Bob Rush of Salida, Mike Swantek of Maysville, and Ricki Santarelli and Glenn George of Gunnison were most generous in providing pictures of the South Arkansas and Marshall Pass regions.

Fred Schmalz of Gunnison, George Means of the upper Tomichi Valley, and the Upper Tomichi Historical and Community Association were extremely helpful in providing photographs and information on White Pine, Sargents, Tomichi, and North Star on the Western Slope of Monarch Pass.

I would like to particularly thank Dick Dixon and Gerald Berry of Salida for their great contributions in providing pictures and information. Dixon was of tremendous help on the chapter on the Denver and Rio Grande Railroad. Gerald Berry's family owned the Monarch Ski area for many years, and he was invaluable with pictures and information on the chapters dealing with Monarch Pass and the ski area.

Unless otherwise noted, the images in the book are taken from the author's collection. Additional images appear courtesy of Amon Carter Museum (AC), Paul Brinkerhoff (PB), Colorado Historical Society (CHS), Denver Public Library (DPL), Dick Dixon (DD), Gerald Berry (GB), Glenn George (GG), Will Hicks (WH), George Means (GM), Monarch Mountain (MM), Ricki Santarelli (RS), Fred Schmalz (FS), Virgil Templeton (VT), and the Upper Tomichi Historical and Community Association (UTCHA).

Through the years, my interviews with old-timers like Joe and Pearl Wright, Art Pearson, Raleigh and Margaret Flick, Rial Lake, Bob Arnold, and many others have added immeasurably to the information in this book. History papers written by Western State College students Darrell Arnold, John Dwire, Judy Hollingshead, John Jenkins, Tom McConnell, and David Wiens were also of great value to me.

I am very grateful for the support, guidance, wisdom, and expertise of my editor Jerry Roberts and Arcadia Publishing. Most instrumental in my work on *Around Monarch Pass* was Pam Williams, of historical Island Acres in Gunnison, who scanned all the photographs in this book. Her expertise and advice were of critical importance to me. Lastly, I thank the people from the special place where I grew up—St. Nicholas, a small Belgian farming community in the Upper Peninsula of Michigan—for their inspiration.

INTRODUCTION

Straddling Colorado's Continental Divide in the south central section of the state is majestic and rugged Monarch Pass, towering 11,312 feet into the sky. The pass divides the headwaters of the South Arkansas River, which flows east, and the headwaters of Agate and Tomichi Creeks, which flow to the west. The pass and nearby Monarch Mountain Ski Area are annually blanketed with an average of 350 inches of snow. Monarch Pass and nearby Marshall Pass were the two major entries into the much-publicized and booming Gunnison Country mining region in the late 1870s and early 1880s. From Poncha Springs, five miles from where the South Arkansas meets the mighty Arkansas River, to the top of Monarch Pass is 22 miles. From Sargents on Tomichi Creek on the western side of the Continental Divide it is 10 miles to the pass.

Early travel over Monarch Pass was slow, difficult, and dangerous. Long lines of burros or "jack trains" were the first to make their way across the divide carrying supplies or mineral wealth. The burros were followed by stage lines that brought in passengers and express, but only during summer and fall because of the heavy snow and mud. In the early 1880s, the Denver and Rio Grande Railroad ran up the South Arkansas River to within five miles of Monarch Pass to tap rich silver deposits, and later to gather great quantities of limestone. In 1881, the narrow-gauge Rio Grande became the first railroad to cross the Continental Divide in Colorado when it breached nearby Marshall Pass and entered the rich Gunnison Country.

Rich mining towns sprang up on both the Eastern and Western Slopes of Monarch Pass in the late 1870s and early 1880s. Poncha Springs, Maysville, and Arbourville on the eastern side of Monarch Pass became important railroad, stage, and supply centers. Garfield and Monarch, also on the eastern side of the pass, became booming mining camps. On the western side of Monarch Pass in the upper Tomichi Valley, the rich silver camps of White Pine, North Star, and Tomichi drew in thousands of prospectors. Sargents, at the base of both Monarch and Marshall Passes, served as a Denver and Rio Grande Railroad hub as well as a supply and ranching center.

The great silver panic of 1893, which greatly reduced the price of sliver, marked the end of the mining camps around Monarch Pass and greatly reduced traffic on the Denver and Rio Grande Railroad. However, the railroad over Marshall Pass survived until 1955 by carrying coal from the mines of Crested Butte. The Monarch branch of the Rio Grande lasted until 1981 by carrying limestone from the great quarry at Monarch to the Colorado Fuel and Iron Company's steel mills in Pueblo.

Three separate Monarch passes have existed since 1879. Old, Old Monarch Pass was built during the start of the mining boom and lasted until 1921. The pass was used by miners heading for the Gunnison Country and by the Barlow and Sanderson Stageline. Old, Old Monarch Pass crossed the divide at 11,523 feet and was never more than a rough wagon road.

Because of the coming of the automobile and the ensuing demand for a better road, Old, Old Monarch Pass was replaced by Old Monarch Pass in 1921. The new pass was lower at 11,375 feet, and the road over it cost $204,000. The road ran through today's Monarch Mountain Ski Area and dropped into the upper Tomichi Valley. In 1939, despite a clamor by locals from the South Arkansas and Gunnison Countries to build a road over nearby and lower (10,846 feet) Marshall Pass, a third road was built over Monarch Pass. The New Monarch Pass crossed the divide at 11,312 feet and was built for $1,459,000. Today Highway 50, also referred to as "the Rainbow Route," crosses Monarch Pass and runs coast to coast across the country.

When new Highway 50 was built over Monarch Pass, the crossing became the logical place to develop a ski area. Although local people from Salida and Gunnison had been skiing on Monarch Pass for a number of years, there were no facilities, and skiers could only access the mountain slopes by hiking or by shuttling via automobiles. During the summer of 1939, the Salida Winter Sports Club, U.S. Forest Service, and the New Deal's Works Progress Administration cut ski runs and constructed a rope tow and small warming house—and the Monarch Ski Area was born. The ski area was located two miles from the top of the pass on the Eastern Slope. From this spartan beginning, the Monarch Ski Area became a major ski destination in Colorado, with 183,000 skier visits annually by 2010.

Today over 800,000 cars and trucks cross Monarch Pass every year, and the area has become a winter and summer playground. Nearby hot springs, the award-winning Mountain Spirit Winery at Maysville, outstanding hunting and fishing, and world-class mountain bike trails along the Monarch Crest bring thousands of people a year to the Monarch area. These activities, coupled with the Monarch Mountain Ski Area have made the Monarch region a wonderland. Miners, engineers, visionaries, skiers, and railroaders—all with dreams—made the Monarch Country what it is today.

One

MONARCH MOUNTAIN

UNCHARTED TERRAIN

Over four decades ago, pioneers with vision carved out what has come to mean excellence in Rocky Mountain resorts. Monarch. Where quality has become a tradition.

MONARCH

Monarch Ski Resort Garfield, Colorado 81227 (800)525-9390 In-state (800) 332-3668 Posters $5

A COLORADO LEGEND. In the early 1980s, the Monarch Ski Area created a series of four posters to publicize its mountain. The spectacular posters were widely successful and grace many homes across the nation. All of them featured the same man, woman, and dog and emphasized a sense of adventure. (MM.)

MONARCH ROPE TOW. Two runs were serviced by separate rope tows when the Monarch Ski Area opened in late 1939. One run was the famed Gun Barrel, which was very steep and narrow and terrifying with a creek near the bottom. The other rope tow, shown here, was called Snowflake and was an ideal place for beginners to ski because of its gentle slopes. (MM.)

CALL OF THE POWDER. The Monarch Ski Area is known for its great powder skiing. The area averages 350 inches of snow a year, and its nearly 12,000-foot elevation creates dry and light powder conditions. Monarch Mountain offers some of the finest snowcat skiing (where trails are accessed by snowcat vehicles rather than ski lifts) in the nation, with its steep terrain and huge bowls. (MM.)

MONARCH PARKING LOT, 1940S. With Highway 50 and the Monarch Crest behind them, early skiers have parked their cars just off the road and are trudging to the Inn Ferno Warming House in the 1940s. On weekends, it was not uncommon for the shoulder of Highway 50 to be the parking lot. (MM.)

THE GUN BARREL. The Gun Barrel was the first lift at the Monarch Ski Area when it opened with a rope tow in 1939. Because of its steepness, the run was known was "Bloody Ridge" and became one of the most legendary runs in Colorado. A creek ran near the bottom of the Gun Barrel and early in the season, skiers had to jump over the creek or get wet, which many did. Here local Mike Ley has survived the run in 1976. (MM.)

11

PRE-MONARCH DAYS. Locals skied on Monarch and Marshall Passes before the advent of the Monarch Ski Area in 1939. After a long hike near the top of the Continental Divide, this Salida woman poses for a picture before heading down the mountain with primitive skis and bindings and a guide pole. (MM.)

MONARCH RACERS. The Monarch family of professional ski racers poses for a picture. From left to right, Jarle, Marita, Stein, and Edwin Halsnes of Norway made up a racing team sponsored by the Monarch Ski Area in the 1970s. They hoped to become the most successful skiing family in the world. However, the professional race circuit never caught on, and the Halsnes family returned to Norway. (MM.)

FIRST MONARCH SNOWCAT TOUR. In January 1990, the Monarch Ski Area took advantage of some of the finest backcountry terrain in Colorado. This photograph shows the first snowcat tour in the backcountry north of the ski area. J. W. Wilder is the guide for six people who rode in the snowcat. Customers paid $40 a day or $10 for one run. The name of the operation was Great Divide Tours. (MM.)

POWDER SKIING. Three local skiers from Salida get ready for a great powder day in 1939, the first year the Monarch Ski Area opened. The skis were long and heavy, as were the early poles with huge baskets on the bottom. (Wally Koster collection.)

GUN BARREL. Two-man handsaws and double-bladed axes were used to carve out the first and most famous of all of Monarch's runs. Here two locals ski boot-deep powder on the Gun Barrel in the 1950s. The run's steep pitch and perfect fall line created its reputation. (MM.)

14

Ski Pin. As part of an extensive marketing campaign in the 1960s, the Monarch Ski Area designed a pin with an elderly gentleman resembling Santa Claus on skis. The pin proved to be popular, prompting greater awareness of Monarch. (GB.)

Rustic Ski Lodge. This beautiful log lodge at Monarch, constructed in 1939, was the original building at the ski area. Here, on a beautiful clear spring day in the 1950s, skiers have finished a lunch of hot dogs and coffee and are ready for some afternoon sun and fun. (MM.)

A Unique Chairlift. The Garfield chairlift opened at Monarch during the winter of 1961–1962. The height of the chairs at the loading area was based on an expected snow depth of 10–12 feet. When snow began to melt around the bottom terminal in the spring, chairs were too high to load, necessitating this loading platform that was very difficult to side-step up. (MM.)

Denver and Rio Grande Special. On February 13, 1938, the Denver and Rio Grande ran a special ski train to the top of Marshall Pass, not far from Monarch Pass. Some 408 people rode the train from Salida, 157 from Gunnison, and 122 rode the regular train to the summit. Instructors gave lessons on the top of the pass, and many people took toboggans and sleds for equipment. (DD.)

WOODEN CHAIR. This simple but effective lift carried skiers to the top of Monarch Ski Area in the 1960s. In the background is the majestic Sawatch Mountain Range, which features 15 mountains 14,000 feet or higher, presenting a stunningly beautiful view. (MM.)

NEW WARMING HOUSE. The old 1,100-square-foot Inn Ferno Warming House was replaced by the new 5,500-square-foot lodge for the 1963–1964 ski season. The first floor was available for that season, but the second floor was not finished until the summer of 1964. Cars parked between the lodge and ski lifts, as well as on Highway 50, during peak times of the ski season. (MM.)

DENVER AND RIO GRANDE SKI TRAIN. On February 13, 1938, two special Denver and Rio Grande ski trains left Salida and Gunnison for the top of Marshall Pass to publicize a possible winter sports area; 408 people left from Salida and 122 from Gunnison. Activities included a one-and-a-half-mile race, tobogganing, and ski instruction. People skied the west side of the pass, and the Denver and Rio Grande made three trips back to the summit as a lift for the skiers.

INN FERNO. The original warming house at the Monarch Ski Area was called the Inn Ferno after Salida mayor Claude Ferno, who was instrumental in getting the Forest Service permit and Works Progress Administration (WPA) funding for Monarch in 1939. The warming house was built out of logs and was 30 feet by 30 feet. Heat was provided by a fireplace and a wood-burning stove. The only restroom facilities were the convenient trees around the area. (MM.)

SPRING SKIING. In the spring of 1940, the first year of the Monarch Ski Area's existence, a local skier turns on one of the few runs available then. The skis were wooden and over eight feet long, and the ski poles were heavy. In spite of the spartan conditions, this skier is having a wonderful time. (MM.)

19

SKI MONARCH. The Monarch Ski Area, located just below the pass on the east side of the Continental Divide, is one of the oldest in Colorado and dates to 1939. This 1980s advertisement touts Monarch as an area that could easily be reached by private plane. (MM.)

TORCHLIGHT PARADE. A long line of skiers holding torches makes its way down the Hall's Alley run at the Monarch Ski Area on January 1, 1982. Shown in front is the counterweight to the Breezeway lift. The torchlight parade was a tradition that celebrated the start of a new year. (MM.)

SLEIGH RIDE. George Wadsworth and his team of horses pull an old sleigh with paying customers on a tour near Garfield in 1982. The sleigh rides proved to be very popular and resembled winter transportation of days gone by. Norman Rockwell would have been proud of this portrait. (MM.)

THE MONARCH BACKCOUNTRY. Monarch Backcountry Snowcat Tours began in 1990 and included some of the most beautiful and challenging powder skiing in Colorado. The terrain is never-ending and features 20 to 30 different runs. One of the top backcountry runs is the fantastic No Name Bowl, which can take skiers 2,000 vertical feet to near White Pine on the Western Slope. (MM.)

ALOFT AT MONARCH. Monarch Ski Area employees Jim Brush, Rich Morehead, and Bill Block soar above a Mazda automobile in 1981. The three men did the jump as part of a Mazda television commercial near the Monarch parking lot. It took 15 jumps to get the perfect take. (MM.)

Two

MONARCH
MINING CAMP AND PASS

MONARCH, EARLY 1880s. Monarch, first called Chaffee City, was located near the head of the South Arkansas River five miles east of Monarch Pass. The mining camp was originally named for Colorado senator Jerome Chaffee, but by 1883 the name was changed to Monarch after the nearby Monarch Mine. (CHS.)

MONARCH, 1884. By 1884, Monarch was beginning to boom. From a population of 100 in 1879, the mining camp now boasted 1,000 residents and had rich mines like the Columbus, Monarch, Silent Friend, and Madonna. Four stores, three saloons, and two hotels handled the rowdy miners. (DPL.)

MONARCH'S AERIAL TRAM. Here the promising mining camp of Monarch is stretched out in a narrow line of buildings in 1884. An aerial tram 2,736 feet long and at an elevation of over 11,000 feet carried ore from the Madonna Mine down to the Denver and Rio Grande Railroad far below. (DPL.)

24

ADVERTISING THE MADONNA. Following the closing of the great Madonna Mine for the final time in 1953, its owners did a brisk business conducting tours. The Madonna, located on the south side of Monarch Camp, produced over $14 million of silver, gold, lead, and zinc during its operation. (MM.)

The Madonna Mine

Travel 1500 ft into the mine that produced over $14 million in gold AND silver!

Tours every 20 minutes on a modern electric train!

OPEN DAILY
MAY-SEPT.
(303) 539-4600

EASTERN CREST OF THE CONTINENTAL DIVIDE ON U.S. 50 —
½ mi. west of Ski Town Lodge

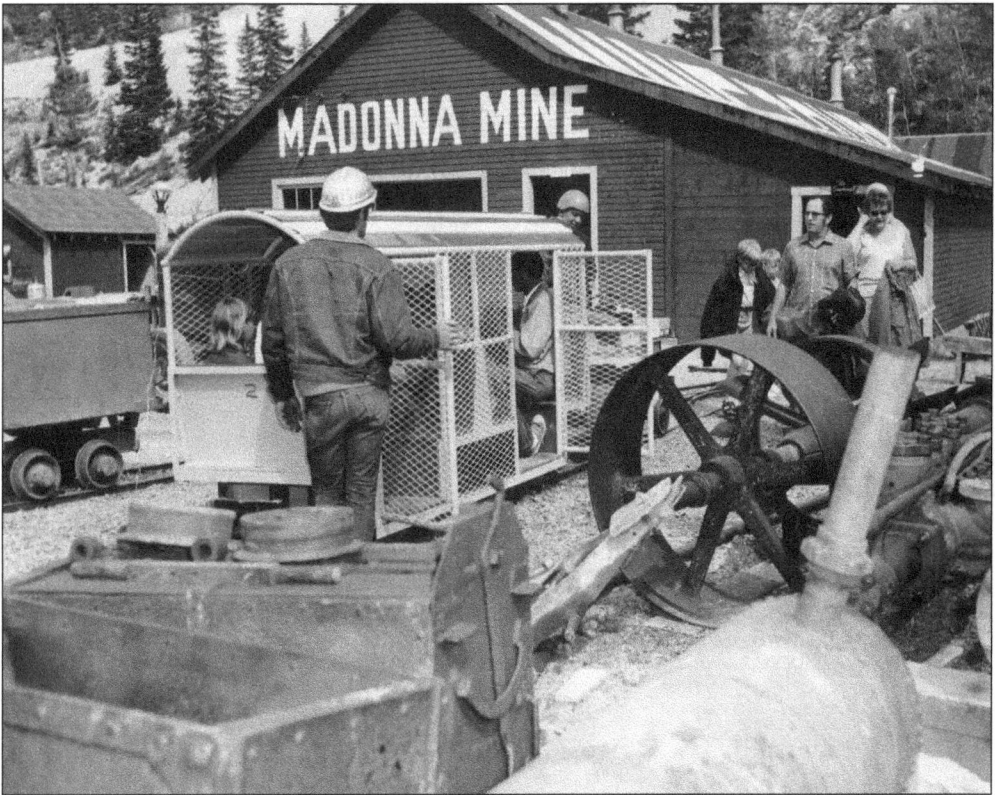

ELECTRIC MADONNA MINE TRAIN. Mining machinery surrounds a modern electric train taking tourists into the Madonna Mine. The tour took people 1,500 feet into the mine. The damp and cold underground mine gave the tourists a real appreciation of the conditions early miners faced. (MM.)

BEGINNING OF MONARCH, 1879. In 1878, the Monarch Mine was discovered by Nicolas Creede, who later went on to great fame with his mineral discoveries near the head of the Rio Grande River. He sold the mine the following year, believing it to contain only low-grade ore. In this photograph, the early tents and cabins of the camp are visible, along with the damaging effects of a recent fire. (DPL.)

THE MINE THAT MADE MONARCH FAMOUS. The Madonna Mine, shown here in the 1880s, was found in 1878 by prospectors George Smith and Mark Cray. More than $10 million of silver and gold was mined, and the Monarch mining camp boomed because of the strike. The mine never had a mill, as the ore was shipped to a smelter in Pueblo via the Denver and Rio Grande Railroad. (DPL.)

STREET SCENE MONARCH. After a promising start with a bright future, Monarch collapsed from the silver panic of 1893, which depressed the price of the metal. The mines closed, investors stopped coming, and the population drifted away. As the years passed, buildings collapsed and avalanches took their toll. (DPL.)

EARLY MONARCH. Monarch had once been a booming mining camp along the South Arkansas River. With a population of over 1,000 by the mid-1880s, the camp had a busy red-light district complete with saloons, gambling, and prostitution. By the turn of the century, the collapse of silver prices put an end to Monarch's great days. (DD.)

MADONNA MINE. Long after the Madonna Mine closed in 1953, tours were conducted 1,500 feet into the mine by an electric train. The mine had shipped 30 carloads of ore daily during its heyday in the 1880s. The silver panic of 1893 ended to the glory days of the Madonna. (MM.)

MONARCH QUARRY. In the 1930s, the Colorado Fuel and Iron Company from Pueblo bought the property of the old Madonna Mine and nearby land and developed it into the largest limestone quarry in Colorado. The limestone was used in the production of steel in the mills of Pueblo. (DD.)

TOP OF THE WORLD. Two new automobiles rest on top of Monarch Pass in the 1920s in a Salida advertisement. The pass was primitive and the dirt road was impassible in winter and difficult during spring months. Sensible people took the Denver and Rio Grande train over nearby Marshall Pass, which was 500 feet lower in elevation.

ON MONARCH PASS. Edith Carlson and her niece Dorothy pose on top of Monarch Pass in 1942. Garfield and Salida are on the east side of the divide and Gunnison and Sargents on the west side. Highway 50, called the Rainbow Route because of how it arched over Monarch Pass, ran cross-country from the Atlantic to the Pacific.

MONARCH, 1924. By 1924, Monarch had become a near ghost town with only a few residents. The great days when it had a mining exchange, assay office, the Palace of Pleasure, Eureka Dance Hall, and rich silver and gold mines were over. The good times were all gone. (DD.)

TOUGH GOING ON MONARCH PASS. Lily McGraw and son Mac, of Gunnison, are pictured on the west side of Monarch Pass in the 1930s. The pass has just been opened in the late fall after a major snowstorm. The road is narrow and muddy and both mother and son are relieved to know that the bottom of the pass is near. (Mac McGraw collection.)

MONARCH PASS, WESTERN SLOPE. Monarch Pass, across the Continental Divide, is the story of three separate passes: Old, Old Monarch; Old Monarch; and Monarch. A primitive road was built over Old, Old Monarch Pass in 1879 at 11,523 feet. The pass was constructed to connect the South Arkansas River camps on the east side of the divide with the upper Tomichi camps on the west side.

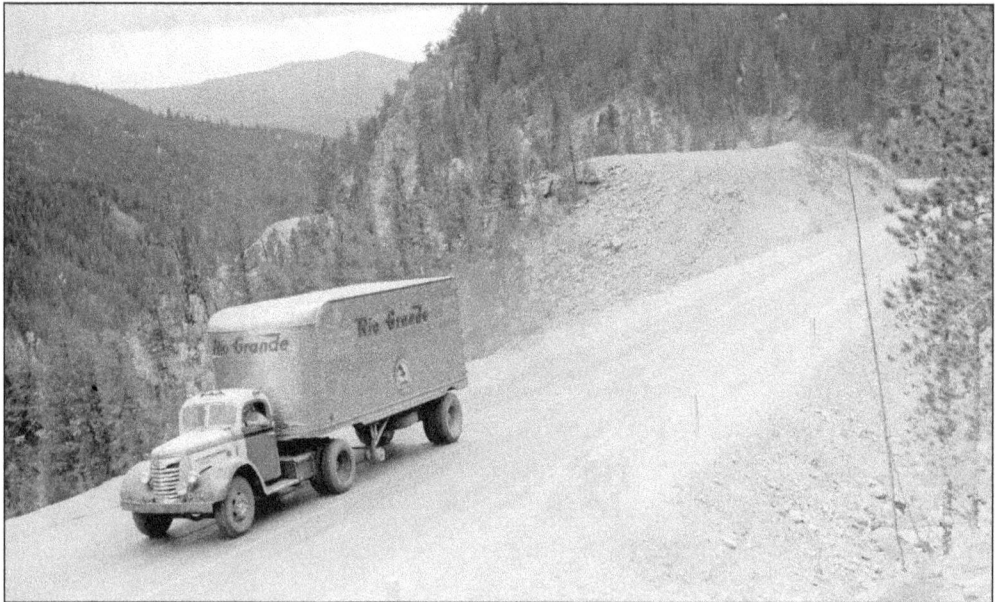

RIO GRANDE EXPRESS. A Rio Grande Motorways truck heads down the east side of Monarch Pass in the 1950s. When the Denver and Rio Grande Railroad ended operations over Marshall Pass, the more direct Monarch Pass was used for shipping. The Monarch Pass road had few safety precautions, such as guardrails and truck turnouts, at that time. (DPL.)

MONARCH SLIDE, 1907. A roaring avalanche in 1907 wiped out many of Monarch's buildings. Only a few residents remained from the 1,000 who had once lived there. After the silver panic of 1893, buildings were torn down for fuel and the post office closed in 1904. Highway construction along Highway 50 further reduced the town to a few buildings and a schoolhouse. By 1907, little remained of the old mining camp. (DD.)

MONARCH, 1907. Monarch's great days were long gone by 1907. The silver panic of 1893 and the rugged winters had seen to that. However, the nearby mountains held great deposits of limestone, which is essential for steel production. Monarch would soon revive and experience a new boom. (DD.)

VAIL PASS. When Old Monarch Pass was replaced by the new Monarch Pass in 1939, Charles Vail, chief engineer of the Colorado Highway Department, tried to name the crossing for himself. However, Vail was exceedingly unpopular, and locals tore down or defaced the sign. Ultimately, Governor Ralph Carr officially named the crossing Monarch Pass. Today's Vail Pass is located between the Copper Mountain Ski Area and Vail along Interstate 70.

MADONNA ORE PORTAL, 1914. Four miners pose outside the Madonna ore dumps in 1914. The Madonna opened in the late 1870s, and until the Denver and Rio Grande Railroad reached Salida in 1880, concentrates were hauled to the railhead at Cañon City in horse-drawn wagons. The arrival of the Denver and Rio Grande in Maysville in 1881 and Monarch in 1883 ended the transportation dilemma.

SKI RUNS AT MONARCH. This drawing by legendary artist Bill Brown shows the runs at the Monarch Ski Area in the 1970s. The Garfield lift is on the left, the Breezeway lift is to the right, and the beginner Poma lift is in the middle. The Panorama lift, which opened up the most challenging Monarch runs, had not yet been built. The drawing looks towards the west and the Gunnison Country. (MM.)

PLOWING THE PASS. A primitive snowplow clears heavy snow from the east side of Monarch Pass in 1940. Monarch Pass annually receives 300 to 400 inches of snow, which is often accompanied by swirling winds that greatly reduce visibility. Avalanches are another hazard on both sides of the pass.

Three

GARFIELD AND MAYSVILLE

THE GARFIELD BOOM. Garfield was a boomtown in the 1880s. The mining camp featured three hotels, 12 saloons, a dance hall, and gambling establishments. Wyoming Kate was well known as "the Queen of Faro" in Garfield. Crime was common, but vigilante committees meted out severe justice. (DPL.)

GARFIELD, 1920S. The mining camp of Garfield rests tranquilly and peacefully, its great years behind it, in 1920. The camp once had been the trading and social center for the nearby mining camps of Maysville and Monarch. Once wide open and lawless, Garfield had now reached maturity. (DPL.)

SNOWSHOE EXPRESS. Before the railroad came to the South Arkansas and Gunnison Countries on opposite sides of the Continental Divide, mail and limited supplies came in by "snowshoe express." Here a horse pulls a supply sled with a skier (then called a snowshoer) behind in 1908.

GARFIELD, 1886. Garfield was the new name given to Junction City by 1883. The rich mining camp was named in honor of the assassinated president of the United States, James Garfield. Garfield seemed to have it all in the early 1880s—rich mines, a prime location where two main wagon roads came together, and rich investors. (DPL.)

TOWN HALL, 1920. Mr. and Mrs. Lloyd Felton pose next to their almost new Ford automobile with the Garfield town hall in the background in 1920. Nearly 40 years before, the mining camp had the Black Tiger, Columbus, Silent Friend, Mountain Chief, and other rich mines that promised to make Garfield the major town of Chaffee County.

39

MONARCH MINERS' CABIN. Miners worked long hours and lived in spartan accommodations in their quests to strike it rich. Cabins were built out of nearby timber. Coffee, bacon, beans, and bread provided most meals. Very few amenities of home existed, and miners lived lonely lives. (DPL.)

JUNCTION CITY/GARFIELD, 1880. Junction City was laid out in 1880 at the mouth of the middle fork of the South Arkansas River on the east side of Monarch Pass. Rich mines like the Black Tiger and Columbus led to a population of 500 the first year. Junction City was named because it was located at the junction of two wagon roads; one going over Monarch Pass and the other over Alpine Pass. (DPL.)

GARFIELD STORE, 1920. The glory days of Garfield were long gone by 1920. Only a few residents, like the two seen here at a primitive store, remained in the once booming mining camp. A little mining was done nearby, and a few tourists visited the little village. However, fire, heavy snows, and the collapse of mining made Garfield a near ghost town.

EARLY TRANSPORTATION. Pack mules were the means of transporting goods and taking ore out of Monarch in the days before the railroad arrived. Long lines of mules, heavily laden with supplies and operating on narrow mountain trails, were invaluable. Here a string of mules carries supplies brought in by the railroad whose tracks can be seen.

A MINING CAMP ON THE RISE. The year was 1886 and Garfield had high hopes for a bright future. The population in and around the mining camp approached 1,000, and rich mines were being worked. The camp consisted of two parallel streets, one higher than the other, on a hillside. Garfield had recovered from a devastating fire in 1883 that wiped out part of the camp. (DPL.)

MAYSVILLE, 1915. A touring car with out-of-state tourists makes its way through Maysville and by its historic schoolhouse in 1915. The one-room schoolhouse took in children from Monarch all the way to near Poncha Springs. (DPL.)

MAYSVILLE BAND, 1880. Every mining camp had a town band, and Maysville was no exception. Most miners came from ethnic backgrounds that highlighted music and dancing. This 10-man Irish band played on weekends and on special occasions like weddings and religious holidays. (DD.)

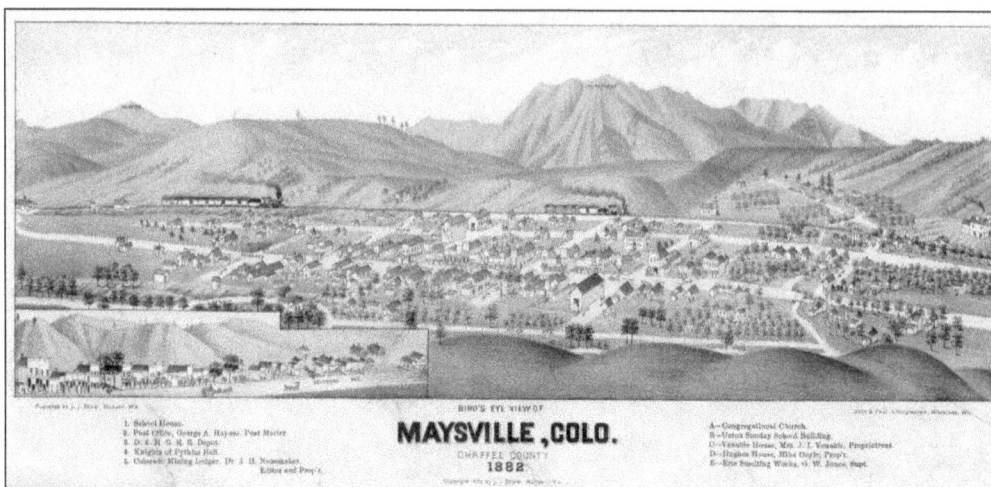

BIRDS-EYE VIEW OF MAYSVILLE. This artist's drawing of Maysville in 1882 shows a well-planned town along the banks of the South Arkansas River. The Denver and Rio Grande Railroad runs in the background, and Maysville is complete with a post office, school, church, and hotels. (DPL.)

MAYSVILLE, 1880s. This photograph looks down at Maysville from the primitive and rough road that ran from Monarch Pass east to Salida and the Arkansas River, shortly after that supply and transportation center began. (DPL.)

SOUTH ARKANSAS COUNTRY, 1880. Maysville, seen here, was laid out in late July 1880. The camp was seven miles down the South Arkansas River from the booming mining camp of Monarch. It was originally a ranch, and its first name was "Crazy Camp" for the wild times that soon came to the region. (DD.)

VENABLE HOTEL, MAYSVILLE. Colorado Avenue was the major business street in early Maysville. Several fine hotels were built to handle the boom of the early 1880s. Mrs. J. I. Venable was the proprietor of this well-built, two-story structure in the heart of the camp. (DD.)

45

MAYSVILLE DRY GOODS. Maysville was named for the Kentucky hometown of William Marshall, the army officer who discovered nearby 10,846-foot Marshall Pass in 1873. The town was platted in 1879, and by 1882 it was the largest town in Chaffee County. (DPL.)

MAYSVILLE SCHOOLHOUSE. This beautiful schoolhouse with its bell on top was built in 1882. The school was used until 1939 by children of Maysville and the surrounding region and still stands today. (DD.)

BLIZZARD DRILL. Maysville children are practicing an unknown "blizzard drill" in 1882. The town was near its peak with a railroad, stage traffic, two smelters, two newspapers—the *South Arkansas Miner* and the *Maysville Chronicle*—plus numerous stores and saloons. (DPL.)

MAYSVILLE BOARDINGHOUSE. The year is 1881, and this pretentious two-story boardinghouse has just been built. Optimism reigned in Maysville because it was the site of the tollgate on the road that led to Monarch Pass and because of the booming silver mines to the west near the South Arkansas River headwaters. (DPL.)

TURNER AND MACY STORE. Miners and children pose in front of one of the early stores of Maysville in the early 1880s. Because of its location on the road to Monarch Pass and its railroad connection, Maysville was a promising camp from 1879 to 1893. (DPL.)

CHEAP CHARLIE'S ST. LOUIS CLOTHING HOUSE. The number-one clothing shop in Maysville was the two-story Cheap Charlie's, which was started by a St. Louis entrepreneur. The store had everything needed to outfit miners headed for the mountains. (DPL.)

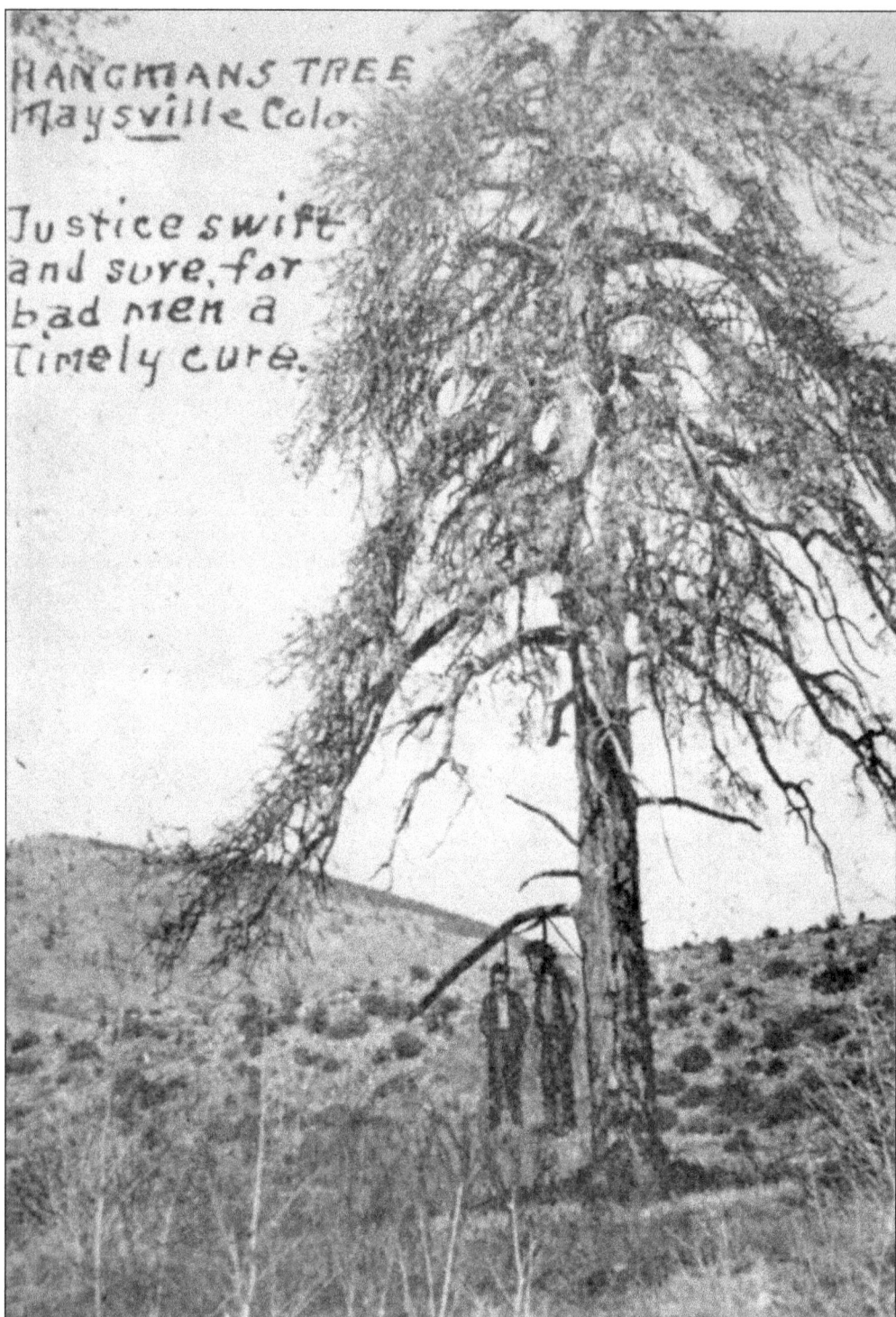

HANGMAN'S TREE, MAYSVILLE. The inscription reads, "Justice Swift and sure—for bad men a timely cure." This hanging tree just outside of Maysville was used to string up several outlaws in the 1880s. Mining camps took care of lawbreakers quickly and decisively. (DPL.)

Four

PONCHA SPRINGS AND ARBOURVILLE

CAMP NEAR PONCHA SPRINGS.
The Poncha Hot Springs
and buildings are shown here
with the town a mile below
in the 1880s. The 55 springs
were reached by wagon road.
The hot springs were 400 feet
higher than the town and
according to one testimonial
were "very beneficial in cases of
rheumatism and diseases." (DD.)

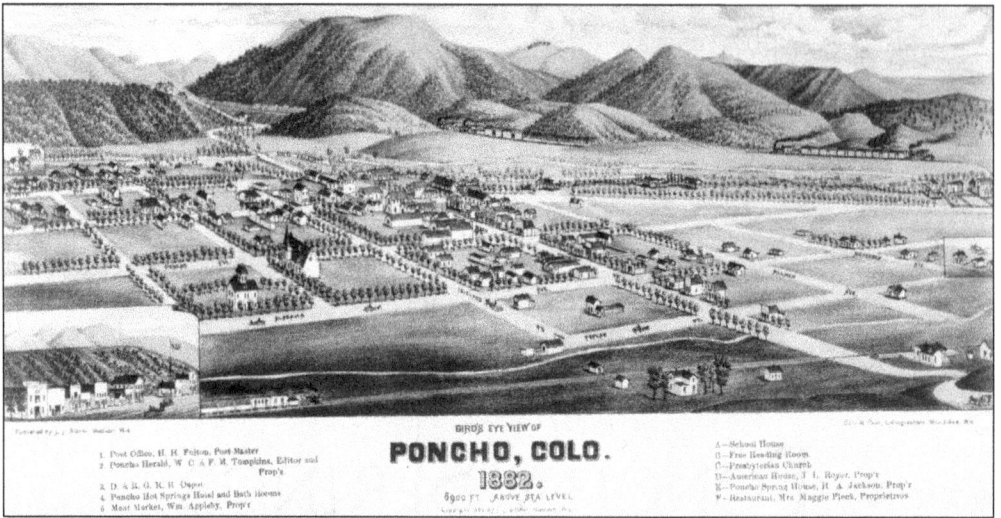

PONCHO, COLORADO, 1882. Poncha Springs was known was Poncha Junction, Poncho Springs, and simply Poncho. This beautiful artist's map of Poncho in 1882 shows the growth of the strategically located town that now had a railroad, newspaper, post office, schoolhouse, and hotel. (DD.)

PONCHA HOT SPRINGS, 1899. Poncha Springs came into existence because of its location on a toll road and railroad route, but also because of its famous hot springs. The springs were well known to Native Americans. Soon after they arrived, white settlers built the Jackson Hotel and bathhouses close to the springs. The springs were located on a hill south of town and some had temperatures of 180 degrees, necessitating the piping in of cooler water in order to be used for bathing. (DPL.)

PONCHA SPRINGS PICNIC. Early Poncha Springs residents gather in the 1880s beneath a wooden gazebo and a series of tents. Picnics were common in the early days when travel was limited. The gatherings featured good food, dancing, and pitching horseshoes, and they allowed people to take a break from their rather isolated and hard lives. (DPL.)

TROPHY HOME, PONCHA SPRINGS. This beautiful home was built when Poncha Springs was in the throes of a burst of prosperity in the 1880s. The town was well established before Salida, further down the valley, was even thought of. The Poncha Springs Hotel was built in 1878 and four years later was renamed the Jackson Hotel. The historic hotel still stands today. (DD.)

BUILDING PONCHA SPRINGS. Poncha Springs was located near the Arkansas River on the eastern side of the Continental Divide. The camp was the earliest in the South Arkansas region. Poncha Springs was laid out in 1874 by James True, who opened a general store to service travelers coming up the Arkansas River from Cañon City or going from the San Luis Valley to California Gulch (later called Leadville). Here a new Denver and Rio Grande depot is being built. (DPL.)

PONCHA SPRINGS SCHOOL. Students and teachers pose in front of a primitive new school building in Poncha Springs. An outhouse is visible on the side of the school. Poncha Springs in the early 1880s was in the midst of a boom. The Denver and Rio Grande was en route to Marshall Pass, the famous hot springs attracted many, and the Jackson Hotel provided accommodations for the weary. (DPL.)

LOOKING TOWARD PONCHA PASS. The new town of Poncha Springs was platted in 1879 and was strategically located. The town was the eastern jumping-off point for the Denver and Rio Grande Railroad as it began its climb towards the top of Marshall Pass in 1881. Poncha Springs also was on the road from Leadville to the San Luis Valley via the 9,022-foot-high Poncha Pass. (DPL.)

PONCHA SPRINGS MEAT MARKET. Poncha Springs experienced prosperity in the 1880s. Here a group of residents gathers around the meat market with the famous Jackson Hotel, built in 1878, in the background. Poncha Springs boomed because of its access to Poncha Pass, its hot springs, and its location on the Denver and Rio Grande Railroad. (DD.)

PRIMITIVE CABIN. Four early residents of Arbourville pose by their cabin shortly after the start of the camp in 1880. Men from Silver Cliff, led by Pap Arbour, saw great potential in the new camp. Great mines were located nearby and the Denver and Rio Grande Railroad was already surveying a line along the South Arkansas River through Arbourville. (DD.)

EARLY ARBOURVILLE. Arbourville was laid out in 1879 by Pap Arbour of Silver Cliff. Arbour intended to establish a stage station on the new Monarch and Gunnison toll road but never did. Instead the promoter built a parlor house in 1880 and did a booming business with the miners, railroad builders, and investors who flocked in. (DPL.)

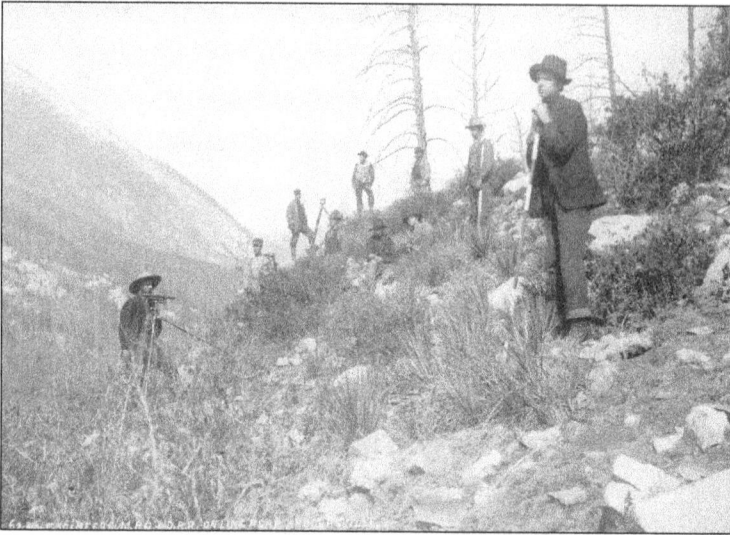

ENGINEERING THE DENVER AND RIO GRANDE. Denver and Rio Grande engineers surveyed a narrow-gauge railroad from Poncha Springs to the new and promising mining camp of Monarch in 1880. The route ran up the South Arkansas River seven miles to Maysville in 1881 and then was extended to Monarch in 1883. (DD.)

THE HERMIT OF ARBOURVILLE. Frank Gimlett, the famous "Hermit of Arbourville," is on the left with Colorado governor Ralph Carr sitting down in Carr's office in 1940. Gimlett was an old prospector who built a home in an aspen grove at Arbourville. He wrote articles on the history of mining camps on the Eastern and Western Slopes of Monarch Pass, the Denver and Rio Grande Railroad, different mines, and colorful miners, but mostly he defended gold and silver. His writings are contained in a series of yearly publications entitled *Over Trails of Yesterday.*

ARBOURVILLE AT HIGH TIDE. The promising camp of Arbourville neared its peak in 1882. A Colonel Steinberger built this house in that year, and the camp had high hopes for its future. However, the mines near the South Arkansas River were located near Garfield and Monarch to the west, and Arbourville soon faded. (DPL.)

ARBOURVILLE, 1880. Arbourville was just getting started in 1880. The new camp was located 15 miles from Salida and 4 miles up the South Arkansas River from Maysville. An early traveler told of "a large encampment of men four miles above Maysville, cutting and hauling timber for houses . . . cutting and thinning out cottonwoods and . . . a surveyor laying off the tract into town lots." (DPL.)

GOLDEN DAYS. By 1881, Arbourville's population had reached 400, and it had a small smelter. The fledgling camp had a post office for little over a year, with frame buildings going up. The Denver and Rio Grande Railroad ran through the camp in the early 1880s, but Arbourville soon faded and was left with only its famous hermit, Frank Gimlett, who had a small home near the river. (DPL.)

Five

WHITE PINE

WHITE PINE TO SARGENTS EXPRESS. A White Pine mother in the late 1800s gets ready to pull her two-year-old son 13 miles from White Pine to Sargents. The mother had a long cord that ran around her wrist to the front of the sled. The trip was slightly downhill, but mom had to be tired after the long journey.

HIGH ALTITUDE HOTEL. The Hotel Rohm was one of the first hotels built in White Pine during the start of the mining camp in the early 1880s. It was located on Main Street, which was the only major street because the mining camp had grown up in a gulch. The backyards of the homes on the west side of Main were 50 to 70 feet higher than street level, and the rears of homes on the east side were 10 to 40 feet lower than in front.

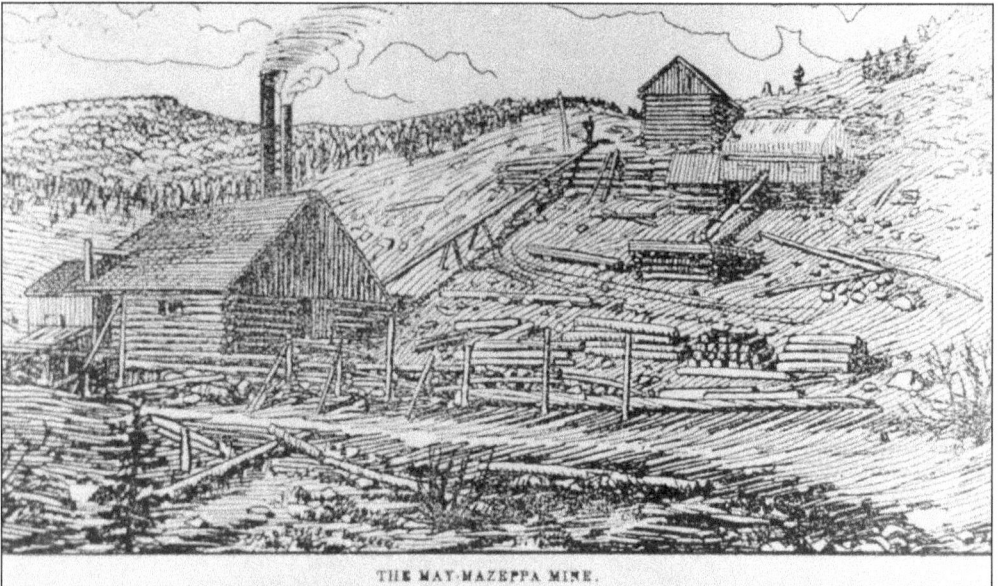

THE MAY-MAZEPPA MINE.

MAY MAZEPPA. This artist's drawing of the May-Mazeppa immortalizes one of the great mines in White Pine history. The mine opened in the early 1880s and produced $10,000 a month of lead and silver. The mine employed its own teamsters, and 11 two-horse teams carried ore daily to the railhead at Sargents, which was 13 miles away. The silver panic of 1893 brought the great days of the May-Mazeppa to an end.

YOUNG SCHOLARS. Five young girls pose in front of the White Pine School in 1884, one year after the school was built. Teachers were hard pressed to teach students from ages 5 to 14 in one building. The teachers rarely lasted more than a year in White Pine because of the camp's isolation, low pay, and rigors of the job. The school term was in the spring, summer, and fall due to heavy snow and subzero temperatures during the winter months. (GM.)

COWBOY AND WIFE. Ernest Means and wife Ida are pictured on their ranch in the upper Tomichi Valley, just west of Monarch Pass, in the 1930s. The ranch was located at an elevation of 9,000 feet, and though the growing season was short, great hay crops were produced, irrigated by the plentiful waters of Tomichi Creek. White Pine was above the Means ranch and Sargents was below. (GM.)

END OF THE BOOM. The good times were all gone in White Pine when this photograph was taken in 1908. On the left of Main Street are a boardinghouse, town hall, and another boardinghouse. Just 25 years earlier, White Pine had boasted a population of 1,000, with rich mines, three hotels, and stage service. The silver panic of 1893 ended the good times. (GM.)

WHITE PINE SCHOOL, 1908. The children of White Pine first attended school in nearby Tomichi until 1883, when this log structure was built. The number of students in this one-room schoolhouse numbered between 20 and 40 students in grades one through eight. If a student chose to continue his or her education past eighth grade, he or she was forced to board out in Gunnison or some other town. (GM.)

LIBERTY BELL. Near the historic old mining camp of White Pine, on the Upper Tomichi River in the Gunnison Country, grows a perfect liberty bell. The bell consists of aspen trees growing amid evergreens. To this point, only locals were aware of this natural phenomenon.

WHITE PINE SALOON. With a population of 1,000 during its glory days in the 1880s, White Pine had many saloons to quench the thirst of its miners. George Root, editor of the *White Pine Cone* newspaper, lamented in September 1884, "The last week White Pine experienced an agonizing time. For two whole days there was not a drop of whiskey in town. Nothing but a liberal supply of peach brandy and bottled beer prevented panic." (GM.)

BASEBALL IN WHITE PINE. The White Pine baseball club and its manager pose in front of one of the log cabins on Main Street in 1882. Baseball was the number-one sport in Gunnison Country mining camps, and exciting weekend games were played against teams from Sargents, Pitkin, Gunnison, and Crested Butte, with much betting on the games. (GM.)

CENTER OF LEARNING. The interior of this one-room school in White Pine is spartan. Local children from grades one through eight were taught by one teacher. There were no individual desks, and a wood stove heated the building. The teacher arrived an hour before the students to fire the stove, clean the floor, and shovel the snow in front of the door. Education usually was excellent and involved reading, writing, and arithmetic. (GM.)

MINING REVIVAL. The Callahan Lead and Zinc Company bought the Akron Tunnel in 1930. The tunnel shipped out over $1 million of lead and zinc during World War I. During the 1920s, the Akron Mine Company shipped 1,000 tons of lead and zinc a month to the Sherwin-Williams paint mill in Coffeeville, Kansas. During World War II, the Callahan Lead and Zinc Company worked around the clock to provide lead, zinc, and copper for the war effort. During that time, the company built this huge boardinghouse to provide living quarters for some of the 50 men employed. (GM.)

WHITE PINE HOUSE. The White Pine House was one of the mining camp's finest and most pretentious hotels. The two-story frame structure had eight rooms, a front porch that was a favorite gathering place for locals, and a bar inside. The White Pine House was the place to be in the booming mining camp during the 1880s.

MUSIC, MUSIC, MUSIC. The White Pine Band poses in front of a mining camp saloon. The band was a popular attraction, playing at dances, weddings, and holidays such as the Fourth of July and Christmas. All of the men had musical backgrounds and were highly sought after by the other miners.

MINE OPENING, WHITE PINE. This mine opening was located near Snowblind Gulch, just a few miles below White Pine. The gulch was named for two miners who had found good-paying gold there in the 1870s but had stayed too long. A blizzard caught them in the gulch, and they became snow-blind and perished. (GM.)

WHITE PINE, 1920s. Virgil and Clara Templeton and children are in front of their modest house in White Pine during the 1920s, when the Akron Mine was shipping 12,000 tons of lead and zinc a year to the Sherwin-Williams paint mill in Kansas. To the right is Emma Williams, who ran the frame boardinghouse next to the Templeton home. (VT.)

SUPPLY TRAIN. The Denver and Rio Grande Railroad ran over Marshall Pass to Sargents in the Gunnison Country in 1881. Sargents, however, was 13 miles from the booming mining camp of White Pine. All supplies for the camp had to come in by horse-drawn wagons or sleighs. Virgil Templeton's four-horse team is seen in Sargents in 1924 en route to White Pine. (VT.)

A WHITE PINE FORD. Ernest and Ida Means pose alongside their new Ford automobile in the 1920s on their ranch near White Pine. Because of primitive roads and no plowing at that time, the car was put up on blocks from November to May, and transportation was by horse or on skis. (GM.)

WHITE PINE CAMP. White Pine was located in a picturesque narrow valley in 1879. Rotting flumes, sluice boxes, and rusted mining tools dating back to the 1850s and before were found in Snowblind Gulch and the upper Tomichi Creek region by silver miners who established White Pine. Most of the silver miners came into the upper Tomichi Valley over Monarch Pass from the South Arkansas region. (GM.)

WHITE PINE, 1950. The Callahan Lead and Zinc Company was still operating in White Pine in 1950, but the end was near. The company had its greatest production during World War II, but mining continued at a high level even after the war. A huge flotation mill was completed in 1947 and continued operating until 1953, when falling prices and lack of nearby demand depopulated White Pine. (GM.)

Six

TOMICHI AND NORTH STAR

LEGAL TENDER. The famed Legal Tender Mine of Tomichi was located high upon the west side of Clover Mountain. It was discovered in 1883 above timberline, three miles from Tomichi. The mine was almost impossible to reach. In late 1883, a narrow, steep, and treacherous road was hacked out up Bonanza Gulch, switch-backing madly until it reached the Legal Tender. (AC.)

EARLY DAYS OF TOMICHI. The fledgling mining camp of Argenta was laid out in May 1880 near the Continental Divide. By July it already had a post office, and a month later the name of the camp was changed to Tomichi. Reporter Robert Strahorn visited the camp shortly after it started and declared, "The camp numbers over 500 men . . . and commenced shipping ore within a few months after its discovery." (AC.)

CUMMINGS HOUSE. The Cummings House was one of several modest hotels in Tomichi during the boom days of the early 1880s. The mining camp also had the *Tomich: Herald* newspaper, a bank, three-story concentrator, and a restaurant. In 1881, a Mr. and Mrs. Dunmire opened a tin pan restaurant and barbershop in a tent. Mrs. Dunmire was the divorced wife of Charles Guiteau, the assassin of Pres. James Garfield.

MAGNA CHARTA TUNNEL. The Magna Charta Tunnel was one of the richest mines in Tomichi. However, the mine was located on the lower reaches of Granite Mountain and subject to massive avalanches. In 1884, a slide wiped out all Magna Charta buildings. A devastating avalanche in March 1899 hit the Magna Charta again, along with Tomichi, killing four people and marking the end of the line for the camp. (AC.)

TOMICHI, 1890. Tomichi was laid out in a spectacular location. On three sides of the mining camp were Clover, Granite, and Monumental Mountains, with crystal-clear streams roaring off of them. The beauty of the region also brought danger. Every spring, avalanches roared off of the mountainsides, threatening mine buildings and the mining camp.

TOMICHI POST OFFICE. Two miners and their mules stand in front of the Tomichi Post Office in 1882. Tomichi was a wild and wide-open mining camp, with violence rampant among the 1,500 miners who streamed into every nearby gulch and ravine in the early 1880s. The camp was located just below 11,979-foot-high Tomichi Pass. (AC.)

TOMICHI AT ITS PEAK. In 1881, the mining camp of Tomichi had reason for optimism. The camp had a bank, newspaper, assay office, sawmill, restaurants, and boardinghouses. An estimated 1,500 miners streamed into the camp by 1882, and Tomichi became known as one of the most violent and wide-open mining camps of the Gunnison Country. (AC.)

MAGNA CHARTA WORKERS. Along with the Legal Tender, the Magna Charta Tunnel was the other major producing mine in Tomichi. One owner and many miners stand in front of the mine opening in 1890. The Magna Charta was northwest of the mining camp and was the greatest producer in Tomichi's history. (WH.)

BUILDINGS OF THE LEGAL TENDER. One of the great mines of Tomichi was the Legal Tender. The mine was above timberline, but the boardinghouses and cabins where the miners lived were located below. Mules and burros defied gravity in making their way to and from the mine. A carload of rich ore was taken daily to Tomichi, where it was transferred to wagons for the 15-mile trip to Sargents and the Denver and Rio Grande Railroad. (WH.)

MAIN STREET, NORTH STAR. North Star began in 1882 as a way to eliminate the long walk to and from White Pine, where miners lived, to the mines a mile away. By 1889, North Star had reached its peak population of over 100 and had a post office, the Bon Ton Restaurant, and two saloons. Two- and four-horse teams carried ore from the mines to the Denver and Rio Grande Railroad at Sargents. (AC.)

NORTH STAR, 1908. North Star, originally known as Lake's Camp, sprang up in late 1878 and early 1879 following the discovery of silver ore. The new mining camp was soon named North Star after the rich North Star Mine. The camp prospered until the silver panic of 1893 but then revived in 1901. The Leadville House and post office were opened during that temporary revival, but soon the decline in the silver market and high transportation costs closed North Star for good. (GM.)

NORTH STAR MINE. The North Star Mine began during the early 1880s, a mile above White Pine. The mining camp was incorporated in 1886. By then, North Star had 20 homes, two boardinghouses, two hotels—the Leadville and North Star—one saloon, and one grocery store. The population of the camp peaked at 100, with the North Star Mine turning out huge amounts of rich lead and zinc. (Don Austin.)

UPPER TOMICHI SKIING. The Petersons, North Star residents, are on their skis and ready for a day's outing in January 1908. Skis in the early 1900s were 9 to 14 feet long, weighed five to seven pounds, and featured a leather toepiece with a four-inch heel block behind one's foot. The Telemark turn (a long, sweeping turn performed by driving one's ski in front of the other) was the only one possible and was aided by a seven-foot guide pole.

Seven

SARGENTS

GENERAL STORE. The J. R. Hicks general store had seen better days by the time this picture was taken in the 1920s. The boom days of the 1880s had long since passed, and Sargents had settled down to the life of a quiet railroad, ranching, and timber community. (WH.)

SARGENTS, EARLY 1880s. The original name of Sargents was Marshalltown, named for William Marshall, who discovered Marshall Pass. The town was renamed Sargents for Joseph Sargent, who had a ranch there that served as a cow camp for the nearby Los Pinos Indian Agency in 1879. Sargent became the first postmaster of Marshalltown, and when local people continued to call the new town Sargents, the name stuck. (UTHCA.)

BUSINESS IN SARGENTS. Steve Watters, Mike Smith, Bob Cole, Tom Bruno, and Art Shaw are among the seven men standing on the porch of a lone business establishment in Sargents in the 1920s. Ads for Coors, Budweiser, and Tivoli beer grace the front of the store. Sargents's businessmen did very well selling to railroaders, ranchers, and lumbermen. (UTHCA.)

SARGENTS SALOON. Sargents, first named Marshalltown, became a boomtown for a month in July 1881 when the Denver and Rio Grande Railroad arrived via Marshall Pass. The railroad camp was an end-of-track, and 1,500 men operating out of 20 grading camps were nearby laying ties. Of the first 14 buildings erected in Sargents, eight were saloons, and they did a booming business. (UTHCA.)

POST OFFICE, SARGENTS. On a beautiful summer day, business is brisk at the Sargents Post Office around 1900. The post office was named for early rancher Joseph Sargent in 1882 and was a social gathering place for miners, ranchers, and railroaders of the region. (UTHCA.)

STRAWBERRY PLANTER, SARGENTS, 1942. J. Roy Hicks built this strawberry planter using an Allis-Chalmers garden tractor with the engine in the rear. His strawberry patch was near Sargents at 8,477 feet in elevation. With Roy watching, his son Carl drives and daughter Eula places the strawberry plants on the planting belt. (WH.)

STACKING HAY IN THE EARLY DAYS. Will Hicks of Sargents stands beside his hay stacker in the upper Tomichi Valley in 1920. Hayfields in the Gunnison Country were irrigated by the Gunnison River and Tomichi Creek, and the hay was stacked in the fields by hard physical labor on the part of both men and horses. (WH.)

HEAVY SNOW AT SARGENTS. Frank Veo, longtime engineer on the Denver and Rio Grande Railroad, peers out of his engine in January 1952 following a major storm in the upper Tomichi Valley. The weather has cleared, but it will be slow going up the west side of Marshall Pass en route to Poncha Springs on the east side of the Continental Divide. (UTHCA.)

JOLLY BUNCH CLUB. With the schoolhouse in the background, the women of Sargents are gathered for one of their many social functions during the summer of 1939. The ladies were responsible for the many dances that were held and were also avid card players and skilled horsewomen. (UTHCA.)

First Schoolhouse, Sargents. The first school in Sargents opened in this log cabin north of the railroad tracks and near the coal chute in 1881. The children were taught by town barber John Hill. Gunnison County paid Hill the princely sum of $80, and Sargents parents paid the rest of his salary. (GM.)

Last Train at Sargents. One of the last Denver and Rio Grande engines pulls into Sargents in 1955. The engine was used in pulling up the tracks in the Tomichi Valley and on both sides of Marshall Pass. Soon the valley would look the same as it did before the summer of 1881 when the Rio Grande first entered. (UTHCA.)

HIGH SCHOOL SCHOLARS. Bus driver Roy Hicks poses next to his school bus with Sargents High School students in the mid-1950s. Hicks was on the road early every weekday morning to collect ranching children from the upper Tomichi Valley and had them at the Sargents schoolhouse by 8:00 a.m. (UTHCA.)

SARGENTS SCHOOL BUS. A school bus makes its way through Sargents in the 1950s after dropping off its load of students at the school. The buses ran in all kinds of weather conditions, as school was rarely cancelled in Sargents or anywhere in the Gunnison Country. Heavy snow and extremely cold weather were normal for the high country. (UTHCA.)

ONE OF A KIND. This strawberry planter was first built out of spare machine parts in Sargents in 1942 by Roy Hicks. The machine worked beautifully, but most local people believed that it was impossible to grow strawberries at 8,477 feet. They were proved wrong, as Hicks successfully produced commercial crops for a number of years. (WH.)

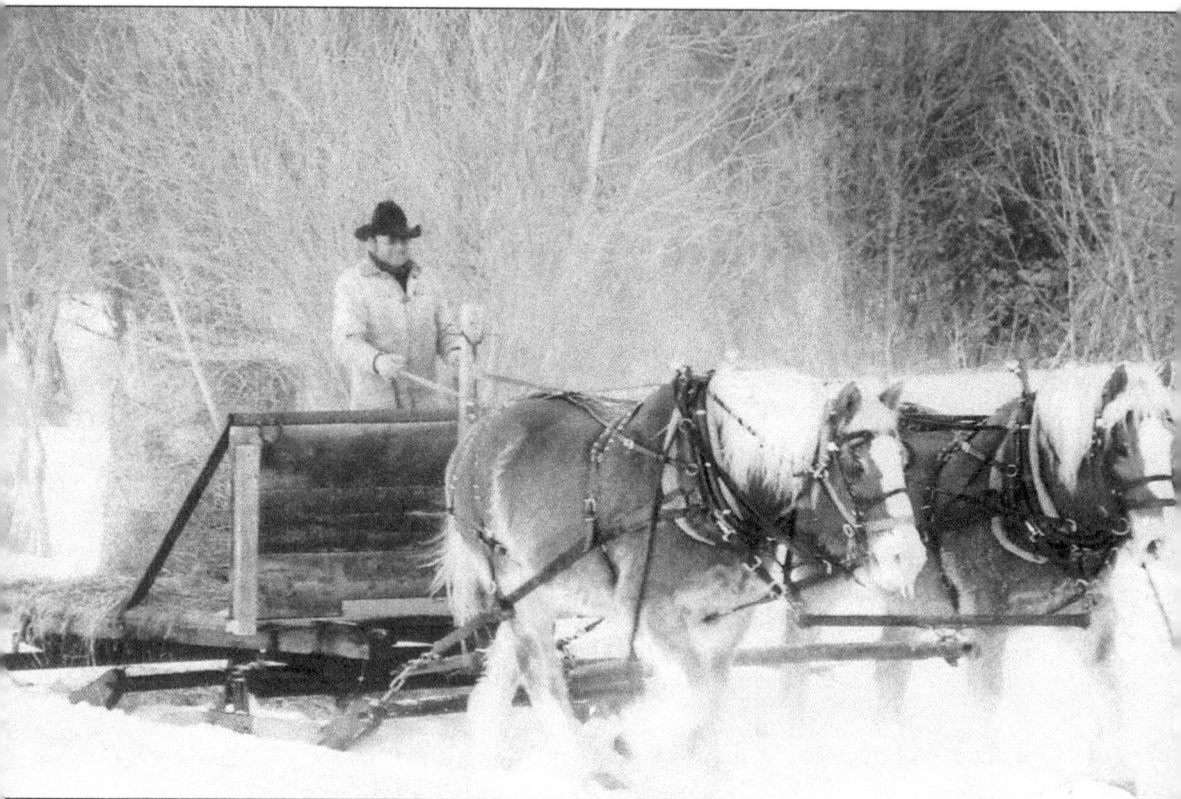

FEEDING HAY, QUARTZ CREEK VALLEY. Rancher Dave Means, seen here on a bitterly cold winter day in February 2005 twenty miles from Sargents, uses a dray on runners to feed his cows. The temperature is below zero as Means guides his Belgian draft horses, Thunder and Lightning, through the snow. (UTHCA.)

Eight

MARSHALL PASS

ENGINE DOWN. The dangers of a mountain railroad grade are exhibited in this scene. The Denver and Rio Grande on Marshall Pass crossed over many washes and ravines that could easily be weakened by spring runoffs or heavy cloudbursts. The grade gave way on this unfortunate Denver and Rio Grande engine in the 1880s. (DD.)

ASCENDING THE PASS. A Denver and Rio Grande engine pulling a passenger train chugs up the east side of Marshall Pass in the 1880s. The grade was steep on both sides of the pass and often extra engines were added to handle heavy loads of freight. (CHS.)

MARSHALL PASS WRECK. Marshall Pass was always dangerous because of its steep grades and many sharp curves. This accident occurred on the east side of the pass between Gray's Siding and Shirley. Derailments and wrecks were more common during the winter months. (RS.)

SILVER CREEK, 1881. The Silver Creek construction camp was located at the junction of Silver and Poncha Creeks on the east side of the Continental Divide. By early April 1881, the Denver and Rio Grande had laid rails to Silver Creek, soon to become known as Shirley. From here it was 12 miles and 2,200 feet to the top of Marshall Pass. (FS.)

WEST SIDE OF MARSHALL PASS. The Denver and Rio Grande Railroad tracks resembled a bucket of worms as it zigged and zagged from the top of Marshall Pass to Sargents in the upper Tomichi Valley. The line gave the truth to the following comment by an early railroad engineer about mountain railroads, "It doubles in; it doubles out, leaving the traveler still in doubt, whether the engine on the track is going on or coming back." (Lois Borland.)

IN THE CLOUDS, MARSHALL PASS. A Denver and Rio Grande engine is safely on top of Marshall Pass in 1882. The Rio Grande gained 3,377 feet from Poncha Springs on the east side of the Continental Divide and 2,369 feet from Sargents on the west side to reach the top of the pass. (CHS.)

MILL'S SWITCH. A Denver and Rio Grande train nears the end of a long climb as it heads up the west side of Marshall Pass. Mill's Switch was a long switchback between the Tank Seven and Shavano Sidings and offered a spectacular view from both sides on the track.

NARROW GAUGE NEAR THE PASS. A narrow-gauge Denver and Rio Grande engine idles near a snowshed on the east side of Marshall Pass in 1882. The Marshall Pass route was only a year old, but it already carried a tremendous amount of traffic and supplies into the booming Gunnison Country on the Western Slope. (CHS.)

BUILDING THE RAILROAD GRADE, 1881. Denver and Rio Grande laborers hack through a spruce forest on the west side of Marshall Pass in this 1881 photograph. Building the railroad grade involved blasting, cutting down trees, and careful engineering. The work was difficult and the hours were long for the laborers, who came from throughout the United States and a myriad of foreign countries. (Bruce Hartman.)

SHAWANO, MARSHALL PASS. Shawano, named for a Ute Indian chief, was on the west side of Marshall Pass. The Denver and Rio Grande Railroad had a siding and water tank there. The Shawano Loop was one of the great scenic attractions on the Marshall Pass route because it offered a 360-degree view of the stunning scenery. Here a Denver and Rio Grande engine heads west just below Shawano in 1907. (FS.)

DOWN AND OUT. Engine No. 241 and several cars of the Denver and Rio Grande are off the tracks and in a ravine following an accident on the west side of Marshall Pass in the 1880s. Danger always lurked on the rails from Sargents to Poncha Springs. (DD.)

SNOW TRAIN—MARSHALL PASS. Multiple Denver and Rio Grande engines labor to pull a train over Marshall Pass in December 1886. The Marshall Pass route was always plagued by wind, which piled up tremendous drifts and created avalanches that roared down steep hillsides. (FS.)

MARSHALL PASS SNOWSHED. Long after the great days of the Denver and Rio Grande Railroad, the many snowsheds of Marshall Pass still stood. The sheds protected against blowing snow and helped ensure the safety of the many trains that passed through its wooden "trough of life." (CHS.)

MARSHALL PASS, 1950s. The great days of railroading on the Marshall Pass route were over following the pulling of the rails in 1955. The top of the pass had once teemed with activity, complete with long snowsheds, a turntable, siding, and lookout tower to check on Rio Grande trains. (CHS.)

MEARS JUNCTION. A Denver and Rio Grande engine pulls a long line of coal cars over a trestle on the east side of the Continental Divide. The coal from the great coal mines of Crested Butte was headed for the Colorado Fuel and Iron Company steel mills in Pueblo. (DD.)

RIO GRANDE LOOP. A long Denver and Rio Grande freight train slowly makes its way around a huge loop on the east side of Marshall Pass in the 1940s. Many loops and curves were necessary on the line as it climbed over 3,000 feet from Poncha Springs to the top of the pass. (DD.)

INSIDE THE SNOWSHED. Snowsheds were critical in keeping Marshall Pass open during winter months. The Denver and Rio Grande Railroad invested much money and manpower in constructing the sheds. Building the structures began in 1881 in an effort to fight the blizzards that plagued the line. This shed was near the top of the pass and was very cold and damp. (FS.)

TOP OF MARSHALL PASS. Buildings and a snowshed dot the top of Marshall Pass as the great days of railroading begin to wind down. Gone were the days when large coal and cattle trains slowly made their way over the divide heading for Pueblo and Denver. (RS.)

TAKING ON WATER. Engine No. 489 of the Denver and Rio Grande takes on water at Tank Seven on the west side of Marshall Pass in 1939. From Sargents on the Western Slope to Poncha Springs on the Eastern Slope, the Rio Grande had 12 water tanks and sidings to help keep its trains running. (DD.)

LITTLE ENGINE THAT COULD. Engine No. 268 of the Denver and Rio Grande heads up Marshall Pass in 1955, helping to pull up the tracks after 74 years of service. Today the engine is the centerpiece of the Gunnison Pioneer Museum, where it draws great interest from tourists. (GG.)

"Galloping Goose" on Marshall Pass. This small "galloping goose" (so called because the engine waddled down the track) from the Rio Grande Southern is pulling rails on Marshall Pass in 1955. The engine originally had been used on the Southern line from Ridgway to Durango. (PB.)

End of an Era. Rails were pulled on the Marshall Pass section of the Denver and Rio Grande in the fall of 1955. Here Jack Brinkerhoff supervises as the rails are pulled and loaded into a railroad car on the west side of the pass. Brinkerhoff and his brother Paul invented a machine that featured cables, a pulley, and winch to pull the tracks. (PB.)

PULLING UP THE RAILS. A Rio Grande Train crosses the highway near Poncha Springs on the east side of the Continental Divide as it pulls the tracks on that side of Marshall Pass in 1955. People on both sides of the pass mourned the passing of a great era. (PB.)

PAUL BRINKERHOFF. In 1955, the Brinkerhoff Brothers Construction Company of Rico, Colorado, received the contract to tear up the railroad tracks in the Gunnison Country and on Marshall Pass. Paul Brinkerhoff, seen here on the right, was in charge of the job and had already pulled up the tracks on the Rio Grande Southern line in southwestern Colorado. (PB.)

A LONE SNOWSHED. The Denver and Rio Grande narrow-gauge railroad raced with the Denver and South Park Railroad to be first into the wildly heralded Gunnison Country in 1881. Key in the Rio Grande's victory were snowsheds on both sides of Marshall Pass, which protected trains from high winds and drifting snow. This lone sentinel was a monument to days gone by. (CHS.)

LAST TRAIN. One of the last trains on Marshall Pass pulls up rails as it makes its way up a four-percent grade in 1955, ending 74 years of railroad history. Many of the rails went to South America to be used on a railroad there, and many others went to the Colorado Fuel and Iron Company in Pueblo. (RS.)

106

DAYS GONE BY. This photograph was taken by Glenn George, one of the Western State College football players who helped pull up the Denver and Rio Grande tracks in 1955. George climbed on top of the snowshed at the top of the pass and took this picture of buildings and cars on the east side of the pass. (GG.)

THE GOOD TIMES ARE ALL GONE. A Denver and Rio Grande engine is going up the west side of Marshall Pass pulling rails in the fall of 1955. Until they had to return to school in late September, 16 Western State College football players pulled rails throughout the Gunnison Country and on Marshall Pass. They worked six days a week, and if they could meet their quota of rails pulled in less than eight hours, they got paid for a full day. (PB.)

THE CREW. These workers, including many Western State College football players, pose for a picture while taking a break from pulling rails on Marshall Pass in 1955. The men were paid $1.50 an hour with time and a half for overtime—big money in those days. (PB.)

Nine

DENVER AND RIO GRANDE

DENVER AND RIO GRANDE BRIDGE. This Denver and Rio Grande engine is on a wooden bridge on the north fork of the South Arkansas River just west of Maysville in December 1896. The narrow-gauge Denver and Rio Grande branch line ran from Poncha Springs to the mining camps of Garfield and Monarch, tapping rich silver deposits there. (DD.)

EXCURSION TRAIN. A Rocky Mountain Railroad Club excursion train crosses a low wooden bridge two miles up, or west, of Maysville in the late 1950s. The train is crossing Highway 50 and is headed up Monarch Pass to its end-of-track at the old mining camp of Monarch. (DD.)

MADONNA MINE TUNNEL. The Madonna Mine was one of the greatest in the history of the Monarch mining camp. Here three miners stand next to a car of ore at level No. 5 of the mine before 1900. In the absence of good smelters, ore had to be shipped to Leadville, Pueblo, or Denver. (DD.)

SLOW GOING AT MONARCH. Heavy snows in the mountains caused an avalanche that covered Denver and Rio Grande tracks in February 1907. Here three locomotives are pushing a rotary plow in an effort to break through. The train has moved only a short distance, and the trainmen are concerned that timber carried by the avalanche may be on the track. (DD.)

MONARCH TURNTABLE. This primitive wooden Denver and Rio Grande Gallows turntable has eight workers engaged in turning an engine around in August 1884 near the Monarch silver mining camp. The railroad branch was then only three years old and was optimistic about nearby silver mines. (DPL.)

RAILROAD TRACKS AND HIGHWAY MEET. A Denver and Rio Grande train approaches a switchback near Garfield on September 25, 1949. Here Rio Grande tracks crossed Highway 50 and brought auto traffic to a halt while the train slowly crossed the highway. Flashing lights warned cars of approaching trains. (DD.)

MONARCH LIMESTONE TIPPLE. The mining camp of Monarch was nearly dead when the Colorado Fuel and Iron Company developed a large limestone quarry there in the late 1920s and 1930s. The original limestone quarry at Monarch was owned by the Eclipse Mining Company and featured an inclined tram from the quarry to the railroad down below. (DD.)

Rails near Garfield. Two narrow-gauge Denver and Rio Grande engines steam just below Garfield in the summer of 1940. An automobile patiently waits as the train crosses the Monarch Pass auto road en route to picking up railroad cars of limestone at Garfield. (DD.)

QUARRY TRAIN. This Denver and Rio Grande engine is pulling 17 empty railroad cars near the Monarch limestone quarry. The engine is only minutes away from backing the cars under the quarry tipple for loading. The cars would then be taken to Maysville, and from there to Salida, for shipment to the steel mills in Pueblo, which was 90 miles away. (DD.)

RIO GRANDE ROTARY. This Denver and Rio Grande rotary is working hard to clear the railroad tracks between Garfield and Monarch shortly after 1900. The rotary was not self-propelled; it had its own steam boiler and was pushed by Denver and Rio Grande engines. (DD.)

MONARCH BRANCH SWITCHBACK. This diamond stack Denver and Rio Grande train is heading westbound and is near the mining camp of Monarch in the 1880s. The Monarch branch of the Rio Grande was narrow gauge and used three switchbacks to go up the steep grade between Maysville and Monarch. (DD.)

SWITCHBACK CITY. The great gain in elevation from Maysville to Monarch forced the Denver and Rio Grande Railroad to use three switchbacks to get to the Monarch limestone quarry. This photograph shows the second and third switchbacks with engine 486 on the left backing up and engine 489 on the right coming down en route to the quarry. (DD.)

LOADING LIMESTONE. Limestone is being loaded onto a Denver and Rio Grande railroad car on August 28, 1957, a year after the railroad had gone to standard gauge. The car man is positioning the car for loading, which he did by gravity and hand brakes. (DD.)

THE RIO GRANDE IN WINTER. This Denver and Rio Grande 2-8-0 engine with its plow in the front is nearly to the Monarch quarry yards during a cold and clear winter day in the 1950s. It will soon pull heavily laden cars of limestone to Salida for transfer to Pueblo and the steel mills there. (DD.)

LIMESTONE DUMPSTER. Pete Cribari operates one of two Dumpsters at the Monarch limestone quarry in August 1957. The limestone rocks were taken from here to a smaller crusher nearby and then were loaded onto waiting railroad cars. (DD.)

MONARCH QUARRY. The Monarch limestone quarry operation is near peak production in this scene from the 1950s. Loaded cars of limestone are exiting the quarry and tipple, and 17 empty cars are being backed in for loading. Two trains a day left the Monarch quarry during peak production. (DD.)

LOADED AND READY TO GO. Some 17 railroad cars loaded with limestone sit on a switch near Monarch. The cars would soon be taken down past Arbourville and Maysville to Salida and then to Pueblo, where the limestone would be used in the making of steel. (DD.)

DENVER AND RIO GRANDE AT THE TIPPLE. Denver and Rio Grande Engine No. 481 is under the Monarch tipple at the limestone quarry in September 1955. The engine has disconnected after backing empty cars past the tipple for loading and is moving out to connect onto loaded cars. (DD.)

SECOND SWITCH, ZIGZAG. This Denver and Rio Grande broad-gauge train in the 1970s is zigzagging at a switch as it backs down to Garfield with a load of limestone. From Garfield, two engines took the cargo to Salida and then to Pueblo. Prior to the 1950s and the use of barrel dumps to unload narrow-gauge cars of limestone into broad-gauge cars at Salida, 300 to 500 men with No. 9 scoop shovels did the work for $3 a day. (DD.)

DIESELS AT MONARCH. Two Denver and Rio Grande diesel power units are backing 17 empty railroad cars into the tipple area at the Monarch limestone quarry in 1968. The tipple had five levels, including two for storage, two for crushers, and the level where limestone was dumped into waiting railroad cars. (DD.)

LIMESTONE TIPPLE, MONARCH. The tipple of the Colorado Fuel and Iron Company's limestone operation at Monarch is seen here at its height. Loaded cars of limestone are ready for the journey to the Colorado Fuel and Iron Company's steel mills over 100 miles away in Pueblo. The many spurs and switches to handle all the trains are visible. (DD.)

122

Ten

POTPOURRI

COKE OVENS, CRESTED BUTTE. If Monarch's quarries supplied the limestone for the Colorado Fuel and Iron Company's steel mills in Pueblo, Crested Butte provided the coking coal. These 154 ovens, made of fired brick and enclosed with stone, were built in 1884 and produced the coking coal that was taken by Denver and Rio Grande train 178 miles to Pueblo.

THE GREATEST. Karl Easterly of Gunnison was one of the greatest early skiers in Colorado. Easterly learned to ski on Quick's Hill near Crested Butte and then at the nearby Pioneer Ski Area. Here he is doing a backflip on long skis in 1938 on Quick's Hill. Easterly is the first known skier to do flips on skis and was featured in early television programs.

EN ROUTE TO ASPEN. Members of the Western State College ski team approach 11,800-foot-high East Maroon Pass between Crested Butte and Aspen in the early 1970s. The lead skier is breaking a foot of new snow. The skiers covered 11 miles from the Crested Butte Ski Area to the top of the pass and then 12 miles downhill to a road that took them to Aspen.

JEAN CLAUDE KILLY. Following his three alpine victories in the 1968 Olympic Games in Grenoble, France, the legendary Jean Claude Killy spent nearly a month in the United States as part of a promotional tour. Killy skied in Breckenridge, Vail, and Aspen and spent part of a day skiing the sensational powder of Monarch. (MM.)

AKRON MINE AND MILL. The Akron Mine Tunnel at White Pine was driven over 5,000 feet into Lake Mountain. The mine produced $1 million of lead and zinc during World War I, and during the 1920s it shipped over 1,000 tons of lead and zinc monthly to a paint mill in Kansas. During World War II, the mine provided lead, zinc, and copper for the war effort, and in 1947 the huge Akron Mill was built. By 1953, falling prices and lack of demand closed the mine for good. (Don Austin.)

WESTERN STATE COLLEGE SKI TEAM, 1961. The Western State College ski team poses for a picture in December 1961. Head coach Sven Wiik is kneeling at far left in the front row. Wiik became the United States' Olympic coach twice, turned out many Olympians, and made Western State one of the top three college programs in the nation. The ski team was involved in many races at Monarch.

PIONEER SKI AREA. The Pioneer Ski Area, along with Monarch, Wolf Creek, and Winter Park, celebrated its 70th birthday in 2009. Located three miles up Cement Creek and eight miles south of Crested Butte, Pioneer had the first chair lift in Colorado. The ski area featured three runs and a primitive ski jump. Pioneer was used by locals from the Gunnison Country and the Western State ski team. The ski area closed following the 1950–1951 season.

BIBLIOGRAPHY

Arnold, Darrell. *Early History of the Monarch Ski Area, 1939–1941.* Unpublished Manuscript, Western State College, Gunnison, Colorado, 1983.

Arnold, Darrell. *The Monarch Passes: Trails of the Rainbow Route.* Unpublished Manuscript, Western State College. Gunnison, Colorado, 1983.

Berry, Gerald. Personal Interview. Salida, Colorado, January 4, 2010.

Borneman, Walter. R. *Marshall Pass.* Colorado Springs: Century One Press, 1980.

Crofutt, George. *Crofutt's Gripsack Guide to Colorado,* vol. II. Omaha, NE: Overlaud Publishing Co., 1885.

Dwire, John. *A Brief History of Sargents, Colorado.* Unpublished Manuscript, Western State College. Gunnison, Colorado, 1969.

Everett, George and Hutchinson, Wendell. *Under the Angel of Shavano.* Denver: Golden Bell Press, 1963.

Gimlett, Frank. *Over Trails of Yesterday,* books 1–9. Salida, CO: Hermit of Arbor-Villa, 1943–1951.

Hollingshead, Judith. *White Pine Ski Area: Recreation for Miners.* Unpublished Manuscript, Western State College. Gunnison, Colorado, 1983.

Jenkins, John. *White Pine: Mining Town Off the Beaten Path.* Unpublished Manuscript, Western State College. Gunnison, Colorado, 1975.

McConnell, Thomas C. *Monarch: Forgotten Silver King of Chaffee County.* Unpublished Manuscript, Western State College. Gunnison, Colorado, 1976.

Simmons, Virginia McConnell. *The Upper Arkansas: A Mountain River Valley.* Boulder: Pruett Publishing Co., 1990.

Trails Among the Columbine: The Monarch Branch of the Denver and Rio Grande Railway. Denver: Sundance Limited, 1993–1994.

Wiens, David. *The History of the Monarch Ski Area.* Unpublished Manuscript, Western State College, Gunnison, Colorado, 1989.

Visit us at
arcadiapublishing.com